2.0 ◁

◁

3.0 -

+ -

◁

4.0 -

Making New Life

Jenny Vaughan

FRANKLIN WATTS
LONDON•SYDNEY

First published in 2008 by Franklin Watts

Copyright © Franklin Watts 2008

Franklin Watts
338 Euston Road
London NW1 3BH

Franklin Watts Australia
Level 17/207 Kent Street
Sydney NSW 2000

A CIP catalogue record for this book
is available from the British Library.

Dewey number: 618.1'78059

ISBN: 978 0 7496 8266 8

Printed in China

Franklin Watts is a division of Hachette Children's Books,
an Hachette Livre UK company.

www.hachettelivre.co.uk

Consultant: Mr David Walker, Consultant Obstetrician and Gynaecologist

Design: Billin Design Solutions
Editor in Chief: John C. Miles
Editor: Sarah Ridley
Art Director: Jonathan Hair
Picture research: Sarah Smithies

Picture credits:
20th Century Fox / The Kobal Collection: 39; A&M University / Rex Features: 36; Adam Rountree / AP / PA Photos: 22; Alix / Science Photo Library: 41; Ancient Art & Architecture Collection: 10 (r); Andy Gallacher / Rex Features: 34; Bettmann / Corbis: 18 (t); Dan Charity / Rex Features: 24; David Burton / FLPA: 09 (t); David Nicholls / Science Photo Library: 37 (t); Dr Najeeb Layyous / Science Photo Library: 21 (b); Erik Freeland/Corbis: 26; Eye of Science / Science Photo Library: 01, 33, 48; Ferens Art Gallery, Hull City Museums and Art Galleries / The Bridgeman Art Library: 12; Geoff Robinson / Rex Features: 20; Hans Reinhard / zefa / Corbis: 14; Image Source / Rex Features: 38, 46-47; ImageWorks / Topfoto: 29 (t), 29 (b); James King-Holmes / Science Photo Library: 28 (t); Jeff Cadge / Image Bank / Getty Images: 40; John Giles / PA Archive / PA Photos: 32; johnrochaphoto / Alamy: 30 (r); Jonathan Blair / Corbis: 37 (b); Jupiterimages / Creatas / Alamy: 15; Mark St George / Rex Features: 35; National Library of Medicine / Science Photo Library: 10 (l); P; Saada / Eurelios / Science Photo Library: 02-03; P; Saada / Eurelios / Science Photo Library: 28 (b); Palace of Westminster, London, UK / The Bridgeman Art Library: 13 (t); PhotoAlto / Alamy: 30 (l); Profimedia International s;r;o / Alamy: 21 (t); Profimedia International s;r;o / Alamy: RUNNER; Reuters / Corbis: 25; Rex Features: 08; Rex Features: 17; Saturn Stills / Science Photo Library: 09 (b); Sipa Press / Rex Features: 16; Skye Brackpool / Rex Features: 27; Steve Hill/Rex Features: 13 (b); STR / epa / Corbis: 11; Wayne Hutchinson / FLPA: 31; WoodyStock / Alamy: 19; Worldwidefeatures.com: 23; Zephyr / Science Photo Library: 18 (b).

CONTENTS

INTRODUCTION

MOST PEOPLE want to have children at some point in their lives – but what if it doesn't happen? Many causes of infertility may now be treatable but, sometimes, issues are complicated and hit the headlines. We read about women giving birth to their own half-sisters, or to children they are not related to at all, or to several babies at once. All this is as a result of advances in the science of human fertility.

▶ Being a parent is something that many people take for granted, but sometimes medical help may be needed.

REPRODUCTION – THE USUAL WAY

With many living things, reproduction happens when a female sex cell (called an egg, or ovum) combines with a male one (a sperm) to create a new life. In humans and many other creatures, sperms and eggs meet inside the female's body, where the young grow until they are ready to be born.

For hundreds of years, farmers have kept male and female animals and encouraged them to have young. However, the outcome could never be guaranteed. Sometimes, the young might not be as good quality as the parents, or young might not be born at all – which could be a disaster for the farmer.

HELPING NATURE

For human parents, problems in producing healthy children can be heart-breaking. It has long been known that there are simple ways to minimise risks: such as staying healthy, avoiding smoking, and drinking only in moderation even before conception (starting a baby). The media goes further, reporting on foods, behaviours or other life-style choices that may affect yet-to-be-born children. Yet, even for the most health-conscious, pregnancy just may not happen, or early tests may show that a developing child could be born with serious disabilities. Medical science cannot solve all problems, and even where it can, a range of difficult questions arise. Depending on the kind of help given, these include very big questions indeed, such as what it means to be a parent, and how much value we place on a developing human life.

▲ Racehorse owners choose the best possible parents for new foals, hoping to breed winners.

▼ Ultrasound uses high-frequency sound waves to build up a picture of a developing baby in its mother's womb.

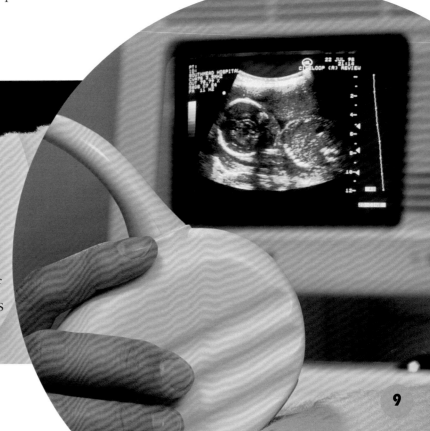

GET THE FACTS STRAIGHT

Ultrasound was first developed in the First World War, to locate submarines. In the late 1950s and early 1960s, Professor Ian Donald at Glasgow University Department of Midwifery worked on the idea of using it to "see" a developing foetus in the womb. This is now routine.

HISTORY 1: MAGIC AND MYSTERY

FOR OUR ANCESTORS, conceiving and bearing children was a mystery – almost magical. They developed a range of beliefs and superstitions around the process. Even today, in many parts of the world, pregnancy is surrounded by traditions and rituals.

PLANTING A SEED

We now know that a baby is conceived when a sperm and an egg combine. But, up until around 300 years ago, the commonly-held belief was that each sperm was a "seed" containing a tiny human being. Some scientists even imagined that, under a microscope, they would be able to see the tiny form of a child. Most people believed that when a couple had sex, the man planted his "seed" in the woman, to develop into a baby inside her womb. The only part a woman played was to provide a place for the seed to take root and grow into a person.

▲ In 1695, the Dutch scientist, Nicholas Hartsoeker, imagined he saw this when he studied a sperm under a microscope.

▶ A statue of the Greek goddess of fertility, Aphrodite.

10

Magic and fertility have always been linked in folklore.

● Almost every ancient culture had goddesses of fertility. In Babylon, she was Ishtar; in Egypt she was Bast, the cat-headed goddess. In Greece, she was Aphrodite (who the Romans called Venus).

● One of Britain's most famous fertility symbols is the Cerne Giant, carved into a Dorset hillside. Tradition has it that a woman who wants to conceive should spend the night on the hill. The carving is believed to date from Roman times – though some scholars think it was made only 300 years ago.

BARREN

If a woman seemed unable to bear children, she was called "barren". (This word is also used to describe wasteland on which no plants can grow.) If a couple was childless, it was almost always assumed that the problem was something to do with the woman. In order to overcome infertility, a woman might try a whole range of remedies, from praying and making sacrifices to fertility goddesses, to drinking potions, wearing special amulets, or seeking the help of witchcraft or magicians.

▲ At the Oshun festival in Nigeria, women of the Yoruba people pray for fertility.

Some traditions still survive, such as the annual Oshun festival in Oshogbo, Nigeria, where people still gather to pay homage to an ancient goddess of fertility. In Europe and America, being kissed under a Christmas sprig of mistletoe may now seem like a bit of harmless fun, but in the past, the plant was an important good luck charm that could help a woman conceive a baby.

HISTORY 2: SOLVING THE PROBLEM

◄ This painting depicts Abraham sending Hagar and her son into the wilderness. Sarah and her son are in the background.

HISTORY is full of stories about people's struggles to have children when this did not happen naturally.

SURROGATE AND MULTIPLE MOTHERS

One famous story appears in the Bible and in the Jewish and Islamic tradition. It tells of Abraham, whose wife Sarah was unable to have children. So Sarah encouraged Abraham to take her maid, Hagar, as a second wife, to bear a child instead. Then Sarah herself became pregnant, and had Hagar and her baby sent away. Hagar can be seen as an example of a surrogate mother.

In the past it was common for men to have more than one wife. This is called polygyny and it continues in many parts of the world today. In societies where having a large number of children is important, rich and powerful men will take several wives and have as many descendants as possible. Often the children are cared for by several of the wives, not just their natural mother.

▲ This 19th-century painting shows Catherine of Aragon, Henry VIII's first wife, pleading with him before the Papal Legate. Henry VIII wanted to end their marriage in order to remarry and have a son and heir.

WHAT DO YOU THINK?

In the past, if a couple could not have children it was common for a brother or sister to send them one of their own children. The author, Jane Austen, had a brother who was adopted by a rich, childless relative. This still happens in many parts of the world.

● Some people think that, in our crowded world, it might be better for childless couples to adopt, rather than use valuable medical resources to try to have their own child. What do you think?

HOPING FOR SONS

In many cultures, sons are especially important. Women who have only girls are blamed – though, in fact, it is the male's sex cells (sperm) that make a child male or female. A famous example of a powerful man wanting to ensure he had a son was King Henry VIII of England (who lived from 1491 to 1547). He divorced his first wife after 20 years of marriage had only produced one child, a daughter, Mary. His second wife, Anne Boleyn, had another daughter, Elizabeth. He soon tired of Anne and had her executed. His third wife, Jane Seymour, did have a boy, Edward, but she died in childbirth. None of Henry's other three wives had children. In the end, all of his children reigned. Edward (VI) died young, leaving his sisters, Mary I and then Elizabeth I, to succeed him.

▲ In the past, people had large families because they had little choice and because they knew some might die in childhood. With a fast-growing world population, is this still acceptable?

THE GIFT OF LIFE: 1

AROUND 100 years ago, a new technique in farming started to be used more widely. This was artificial insemination (AI). It is done by collecting sperm from male animals and introducing it into the females using a pipe called a catheter.

▼ Now that farmers can use artificial insemination to breed calves, there is no need for them to keep male animals.

HUMANS AND AI

Artificial insemination (AI) works for humans, too. For example, a man may have sexual problems, or he may not produce enough good sperm. It may be possible to collect enough sperm, and insert it into his partner's womb. Sometimes, a man may not produce sperm or a woman may want to have a child but have no male partner. In these cases, "donor sperm" may be used

and inserted. This is sperm that has been produced by a man the woman may never have met, and the process is called Artificial Insemination by Donor (AID). The sperm has usually been collected and frozen, and kept in a fertility centre, in what is known as a "sperm bank". If the woman has a child by AI, the father will be the donor, but the child may never meet him.

IS IT RIGHT?

Until the 1960s, most people considered that AID in humans was wrong, simply because it meant that a woman might have a child whose father was not her husband. Today, it is more widely accepted – although some religions, such as the Catholic Church and Islam, oppose it. But even some non-religious people worry about the idea of a single woman, or lesbian couples, having a baby with no father-figure. In 2008, Guadalupe Benitez took her doctors to the California Supreme Court after, she said, they had refused her AI treatment because she is a lesbian. The doctors, who are devout Christians, said it was simply because Ms Benitez was an unmarried woman.

▲ A lesbian couple with their son, who was conceived using artificial insemination.

GET THE FACTS STRAIGHT

Although AI has been widely used on farms for around 100 years, the technique is much older than that. The earliest record of its use is around 1322, when an Arab chieftain stole sperm from a rival's horse and injected it into his own mare, so she would have a champion foal.

15

PARENT PROBLEMS

THE MAIN PROBLEMS around AID centre on the health of the woman and the child, and who is responsible for any baby conceived in this way.

A HEALTHY BABY

When a woman has a child by AID, she might not use a sperm bank. She may use sperm donated by a friend. Doing this can be risky. The woman must be sure that there is no chance of infection. There are many diseases – including HIV and AIDS – which can be passed on with the sperm, and infect the woman and her child. There are also conditions that the baby can inherit, such as muscular dystrophy (see below).

If the woman uses a properly-run, licensed fertility centre she will know the sperm donor has been tested for diseases. She will also know that doctors are as sure as possible that any baby will not inherit harmful conditions that could cause disability or illness.

▼ A young boy with one of the many forms of muscular dystrophy. Some, but not all, forms of it can be inherited.

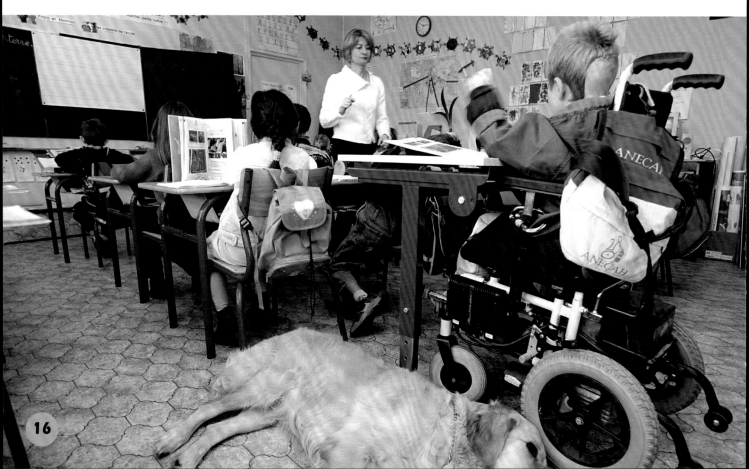

WHOSE BABY?

Sperm donation can create problems. The children involved may desperately want to know who their father is. This is especially important if there seem to be inherited health problems – which is why, in many countries, children now have the right to find out who their biological father is.

Sperm donation can also lead to legal difficulties. Is the donor responsible for supporting his children? In many countries, the answer is "no" if an official sperm bank is used. But private arrangements are more tricky, and can lead to fathers finding they have taken on a costly responsibility. For example, in January 2002, a court in Sweden agreed that a man named Igor Lehnberg must support three children conceived with his sperm – even though he had intended only to help their mother and her lesbian partner start a family of their own. When the couple split up, the mother needed – and won – financial help from the children's father.

WHAT DO YOU THINK?

When a man donates sperm, a good clinic will check for life-threatening conditions he may pass on to his child. Yet some people prefer private donations from friends, for privacy, and to save the costs and tests involved in using a clinic.

- Do you think that private sperm donations should be stopped?
- Do you think this would be possible?
- What arguments could you use to persuade someone to use a clinic rather than a private donation?

◀ British sperm donor Andy Bathie holds the two children conceived after he donated some of his sperm to a friend. Mr Bathie has disputed a UK legal ruling that he must support the children financially.

EXTRA EGGS AND EXTRA HELP

SOMETIMES a woman cannot produce enough eggs to get pregnant easily. Or the tubes that run between her ovaries and her womb may be blocked, so sperm cannot reach them and fertilise them. Sometimes, the woman's partner cannot produce enough sperm, or his sperm is not strong enough to reach the eggs.

▲ Louise Brown, the world's first IVF baby.

MAKING MORE EGGS AND BETTER SPERM

If a woman's tubes are blocked, an operation may help. If she needs to produce and release more eggs, medication may stimulate her ovaries into doing this. She may then become pregnant, either through normal sex, or by artificial insemination. Problems with a man's sperm are more difficult. Medicines and operations have been tried but, so far, without much success, although it may be possible to collect enough sperm for artificial insemination. If nothing else works, a couple may try a method called in vitro fertilisation, or IVF.

The first baby born this way was Louise Brown, from Bristol, in 1978. Since then, millions of children all over the world have started life through IVF.

▼ Implanting sperm into an egg during IVF treatment.

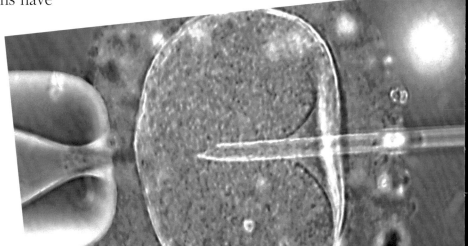

THE TEST TUBE BABY

In IVF, a woman's eggs are collected and fertilised in a laboratory, using her partner's sperm or – if that is not possible – donated sperm. Then fertilised eggs (embryos) are "implanted" (placed) in her womb. If all goes well, at least one will become a foetus (developing baby). Unfortunately, IVF only succeeds around 15 per cent of the time, and is extremely expensive.

In the United States, IVF treatment is not covered by health insurance and costs around $10,000 a time. As couples usually need to make several attempts, the option is really only available to the wealthy. Even in countries with free health care, IVF treatment may be limited. There is another problem, too. IVF may create more embryos than the woman needs, and some may have to be destroyed.

FACING THE ISSUES

Many Roman Catholics oppose IVF – partly because they believe the process itself is wrong, and also because it creates embryos that will never be used. These extra embryos are likely to be destroyed, which the Church believes is the same as killing a full-term baby. Other religions are less definite about this. For example, many Muslims accept IVF, as long as the sperm and egg are those of the couple concerned and not donated.

► Doctors must make difficult decisions about who gets expensive IVF treatment. Does it make sense to offer it to people who do not care for their own health, for example, by smoking?

SAFETY IN NUMBERS?

TWINS naturally make up about one birth in around 100, more in some parts of the world than others. Triplets are rarer – more babies than that, rarer still.

▲ Quadruplets, or quads, only happen naturally in about one birth in 700,000. IVF has made this more common.

MULTIPLE BIRTHS

However, some fertility treatments may result in several eggs being released at once and all may be fertilised. This has made multiple pregnancies and births far more common. In November 2007, a Russian woman gave birth to five daughters (quintuplets) in Oxford. It was only the sixth time this had happened in Britain in the last 40 years. They all survived.

IVF can lead to multiple pregnancies if doctors implant more than one embryo, hoping at least one will develop. IVF often fails, but if a pregnancy does result, around one third of the time the woman may find she is expecting twins or triplets. As IVF techniques improve, doctors are more confident about implanting just one foetus, or two at the most.

PREMATURE AND SMALL

Multiple pregnancies are a problem because the foetuses have to share the space and nutrition available in a single womb. The babies are often born too early. These premature babies tend to be too small, and may have serious health problems. For example, in 1996, a woman named Mandy Allwood became pregnant with octuplets (eight foetuses) after fertility treatment. Doctors wanted to remove all but two. However, Ms Allwood went ahead, and the babies were born after 25 weeks of pregnancy. None survived.

Even twins are seven times more likely than a single baby to die during pregnancy, and six times more likely to suffer from cerebral palsy – a form of brain damage that leaves the child disabled. Of course, many twins and triplets are born healthy – but few mothers really hope for three or more babies at once. Looking after them is expensive – and tiring!

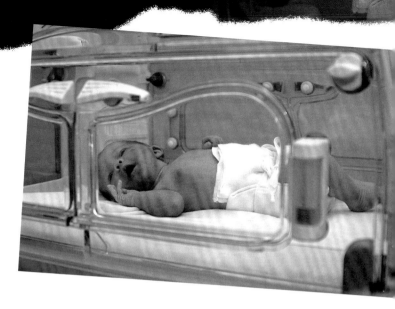

▲ Very small or premature babies have to spend the early part of their lives in an incubator. Multiple pregnancies increase the likelihood of premature birth.

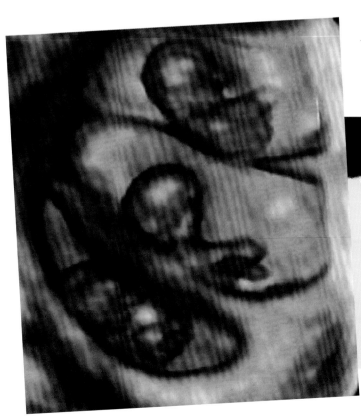

◀ An ultrasound picture of triplets, at an early stage of development in their mother's womb.

WHAT DO YOU THINK?

Some people believe that, if a woman has a large number of embryos in her womb, it is wrong to remove any of them, because that is killing them. Yet, the chances are that they will die anyway if this is not done.

What do you think is the right decision?

JUST AS MEN may donate sperm to help a childless couple, so a woman can donate eggs. It is not an easy process. First, her ovaries must be stimulated. Then she has a minor operation to remove the eggs produced. There are health risks, but some women are willing to make this very generous gift.

▲ US stand-up comedian Jennifer Dziura has donated one of her eggs to help a childless couple. She hopes to donate another egg in the future.

EGG-SHARING

Women in the United Kingdom are not paid to donate eggs (just as men are not paid to donate sperm). But, if a woman is already having eggs collected for IVF, the treatment can be cheaper if she agrees to give some of them away. This is called egg-sharing. It works like this: eggs are collected from Woman A. Some are fertilised with her partner's sperm and implanted in her womb. If she is lucky, she will have a baby. Some of her eggs will be donated to Woman B. They are fertilised with sperm from Woman B's partner and implanted in Woman B's womb. If Woman B has a baby, it will be the biological child of her husband – and Woman A. This raises a difficult question. How will Woman A feel if she does not get pregnant – but Woman B does? Woman A will know that she has a son or daughter somewhere – but no children that are legally her own. In Britain, the child may, however, trace its biological mother.

MOTHERS AND SISTERS AND FRIENDS

Sometimes women donate eggs for friends or relatives. In this second case, the results can be rather complicated. A woman might donate an egg to her sister – so the sister becomes both aunt and biological mother to the same child. Occasionally, a mother donates eggs to her daughter, and ends up being a grandmother and a biological mother for the same child. Some people wonder whether such complicated relationships can actually be right.

FACING THE ISSUES

In 2005, Alex Patrick's son, Charlie, was born. Alex had had cancer, and could not produce eggs. Her sister, Charlotte, was able to donate an egg, but did not wish to carry the pregnancy. So another sister, Helen, had the fertilised egg implanted in her womb and gave birth to Charlie. So who is Charlie's "real" mother?

- Biologically, the mother is the woman whose egg is used.

- The sister who gave birth to baby Charlie was his surrogate mother.

- Alex and her husband will bring up Charlie as their own. They had to go through a legal process in order to be recognised as his parents.

▲ Charlie Patrick with his three "mothers" – Alex Patrick and her sisters, Charlotte and Helen.

TWO MOTHERS?

A SURROGATE mother bears a living child and gives it away. A woman may be a surrogate for her sister, or even for her daughter, as happened in Brazil in 2007. But, often, the surrogate is not related to the parents at all.

◄ The media often reports problems with the relationship between surrogate mother and the mother who will look after the child. Usually, however, the outcome is a happy one – for everyone.

WHY AND HOW?

Sometimes, the "real" mother can produce eggs, but a baby cannot develop in her womb. A surrogate may have the baby for her. Alternatively, the child may be conceived using one of the surrogate's own eggs – often by artificial insemination. This can happen, for example, when a male gay couple want to have a baby to call their son or daughter. The situation can get complicated if either the surrogate or the parents change their minds. The surrogate may feel she cannot, after all, bear to part with her baby. Or the would-be parents may decide they don't want it. Bitter court battles can follow – made all the more difficult if the surrogate and the parents live in different countries with different laws. In Britain, for example, a surrogate is legally the child's mother – but in parts of the United States, this may not be the case.

EXPLOITING THE POOR

In many countries, there are laws to prevent anyone paying a surrogate mother more than basic expenses. However, this is not true everywhere. As a result, a new industry has grown up in poorer parts of the world. In India, for example, many women sell eggs, or even bear children for rich people. The money they get can help pay off debts, send children to school and in other ways transform family life.

WHAT DO YOU THINK?

Many people believe that getting poor women to bear children for richer ones can never be a fair arrangement. They say it is an example of exploitation, and similar to the practice of persuading poor people to sell a kidney or other organ for transplant. What do you think?

▶ Surrogacy has been used in horse breeding for decades. This mare has acted as a surrogate mother for a foal that has a better pedigree (making it more valuable) than herself.

FACING THE ISSUES

Surrogacy can go badly wrong. For example:

● In 1987, a baby called Emma Grace was born in the US to a surrogate mother – who then decided to keep her. Twenty years later, the couple who organised the surrogacy is still fighting for custody of the child.

● In 2001, a woman named Helen Beasley, from Shropshire, agreed to be a surrogate mother for an American couple. Helen got pregnant with twins – but the Americans wanted only one baby. Helen ended up pregnant with babies no one wanted – and they had to be adopted.

TOO OLD FOR PARENTHOOD?

AROUND THE AGE of 50, a woman's supply of eggs runs out. This point in her life is called the menopause and, once she has reached it, she cannot naturally become a mother.

OVER 40...

In much of the developed world, many women are delaying having children. By 2003, nearly nine births in every 1,000 in the US were to women between 40 and 44. In Britain, by 2006, this figure was 12 – a record. But this is risky. An older woman often has difficulty conceiving and there is a higher chance that she will miscarry (lose the baby) or her menopause may come early, so she cannot conceive naturally at all.

There are also health risks. The mother may suffer from high blood pressure, or the child may develop the condition Down's syndrome. This causes a range of medical problems and some mental disability. Men over 40 are also less fertile, and some recent studies have suggested that their children may also be born with health problems. But perhaps the biggest difficulty is that older parents may simply not have the energy they need to look after a small child.

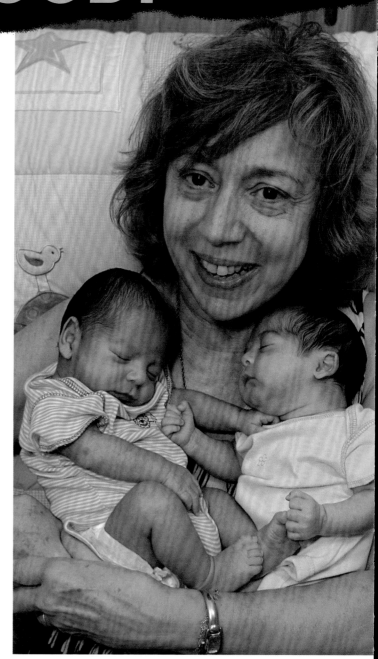

▲ Women in their late 30s and early 40s can have healthy babies but it can be more difficult for them to conceive and there are increased health risks.

WHAT DO YOU THINK?

It is quite common for men to become fathers when they are in their 60s or even 70s. The oldest known father was an Australian, Les Colley, who was 92 when his last child was born. He died in 1998, when he was nearly 100. In 2007, 90-year-old Nanu Ram Jogi, from India, became the world's oldest known living father.

● Do you think it is fair that older women seem to get more criticism when they become parents than men? If the woman is fit and well, why does it matter?

OVER 60...

In 2006, a 62-year-old British child psychiatrist, Patricia Rashbrook, gave birth to a healthy baby boy. Her pregnancy was the result of IVF, and it started a storm of controversy. Was it fair, critics asked, for a child to be born to a mother who would be in her 80s before he was grown up?

▲ Children with older parents can find that their parents are older than their friends' grandparents.

But others asked why we should worry about this. Perhaps, deep down, there is just the feeling that such late motherhood is unnatural and can't be "right".

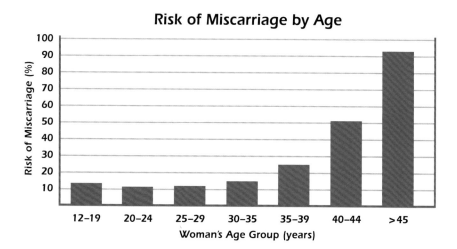

Risk of Miscarriage by Age

◀ This chart shows that, as women age, the risk of a pregnancy ending in a miscarriage grows.

CHECKING PROGRESS

IN THE PAST, a mother had no means of knowing whether her baby was developing healthily. She simply had to wait and see.

SCREENING AND TESTING

Today, each pregnant woman is offered ante-natal tests. These include blood tests to check her health and that of her foetus. If the mother is older, doctors may test the foetus for Down's syndrome. This involves pushing a needle into the womb, withdrawing a few cells from the fluid around the growing foetus and checking them. As the baby develops, doctors use ultrasound pictures to check that the foetus is developing properly. Other tests include further health checks on the mother, and tests to find out if she or her partner are carrying any inherited diseases that may affect the baby.

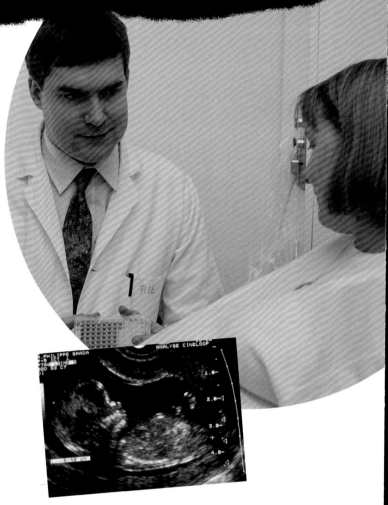

▲ For parents, viewing the first ultrasound picture of an unborn child is an exciting and moving experience.

GET THE FACTS STRAIGHT

We now know that what a mother does during pregnancy can affect her baby. For example, a mother who drinks heavily can damage the growing child, and smoking is also bad for it. In the late 1950s and the early 1960s, a drug called thalidomide was given to women to treat "morning sickness" which pregnant women often suffer. Worldwide, around 12,000 babies were born with disabilities – usually short arms or legs – as a result. Today, doctors are much more careful about giving medicines to pregnant women.

AFTER TESTING

Sometimes, tests show that a baby is likely to have a serious illness or be severely disabled – or that the mother's life is at risk. Parents must decide whether they are able to care for a severely disabled baby, or if it is fair to bring one into the world if it is going to suffer all its life. They may choose abortion, so ending the pregnancy. However, many religious people believe that this is wrong, whatever the circumstances.

Others argue about what is meant by "severe" disability. In 2003, the Reverend Joanna Jepson took her local police force to court, saying they should have prosecuted doctors who carried out an abortion late on in a pregnancy. They had done this because the baby had a facial deformity called a cleft palate. Late abortions are allowed in Britain

▲ Is it better for a woman to have an abortion if her unborn baby is likely to be disabled?

only in cases of serious deformities. A cleft palate is often not very severe – but it can be, and appear with other health problems. Ms Jepson lost her case.

▼ Anti-abortion campaigners demonstrate outside a clinic.

BOYS OR GIRLS?

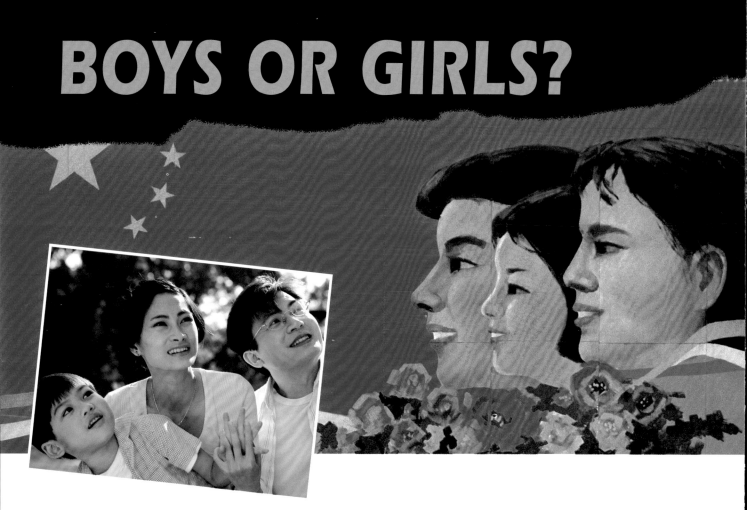

UNTIL RECENTLY, the first question that parents asked when their baby was born was, "Is it a girl or a boy?" Today, there are tests that can show this – and it may show up on the ultrasound.

▲ The Chinese authorities try to persuade parents to value girls with poster campaigns and other education.

A MATTER OF LIFE AND DEATH – OR NOT

Some serious inherited medical conditions affect mostly boys. When this is a risk, parents may want only girls. Some parents may want to choose their child's sex for other reasons – like wanting a girl because they already have boys. In some societies, boys are valued more highly than girls. Girl babies in these societies may be aborted – although it is usually illegal to do this.

In China, couples are only supposed to have one child in order to control the population. Often, they choose to have a boy – and there are around 116 boys born for every 100 girls. About 90% of aborted foetuses in China are female. In India, too, boys are favoured, and an estimated half a million pregnancies every year are ended because the foetus is a girl.

TESTING SPERM

Today there are tests available that can sort sperm into "male-producing" and "female-producing" types – so that the "right" ones can be used in artificial insemination or IVF. These techniques can be used in farm animals – for example in dairy cows, where females, as the milk producers, are much more valuable than males. Using them on humans would avoid abortions – but would still mean societies ending up with far too many men to find partners. In any case, many doctors disapprove of using medical techniques for non-medical problems – like wanting a boy or a girl.

▲ In dairy herds, bull calves are useless and are usually killed. It would make economic sense to ensure that most calves were female.

SAVIOUR SIBLINGS

SOMETIMES a child is born with an illness that can only be treated using material from a brother or sister's body. Parents may decide to have a new baby to help save their sick child. This is called a "saviour sibling" or a "designer baby".

◀ Raj and Shahana Hashmi's son, Zain, suffered from a life-threatening blood disease (see next page). They went to court to get permission to use IVF to create a sibling who could help him survive.

HOW IT IS DONE

The saviour sibling must have body tissues that match the sick child's tissues. So several embryos are created, using IVF, and the one with the right tissues is implanted in the mother's womb. Once the baby is born, special cells, called stem cells, can be taken from the umbilical cord that joins the growing foetus to its mother's womb. These cells can be transplanted into the body of the sick child and may cure him or her. Sometimes, bone marrow from the new sibling can be used as a cure – but this is a more painful and risky procedure for the saviour sibling.

IS IT RIGHT?

In 2003, Raj and Shahana Hashmi, from Yorkshire, won permission from a court to have IVF treatment to create a saviour sibling for their son, Zain. He suffered from a rare blood disorder called thalassaemia, which could possibly be cured by using stem cells from the umbilical cord of a suitable sibling. Since then, other parents have been allowed to make saviour siblings.

Many people feel there is something wrong with creating a child as a source of spare parts. They don't like the idea of destroying the embryos that won't be used – and they worry which "spare parts" will be obtained, and how. Stem cells are easy to collect. Bone marrow is more difficult. Donating organs, such as kidneys, is even more difficult and dangerous. How does the sibling feel if he or she has been created purely to save a sibling's life? The law in Britain now allows this. But there is a move to allow saviour siblings to be created to help treat serious illnesses that are not life-threatening. Is this going too far?

▼ A magnified image of the blood cells of someone suffering from sickle cell disease. Cells from a saviour sibling might help cure this condition.

GET THE FACTS STRAIGHT

Most adult body cells have a special purpose, and cannot be changed. For example, there are cells that make the liver and cells that make the heart. Stem cells are different – they can be made to make any body part. One day, it may be possible to use them to repair a whole range of body parts and cure many diseases.

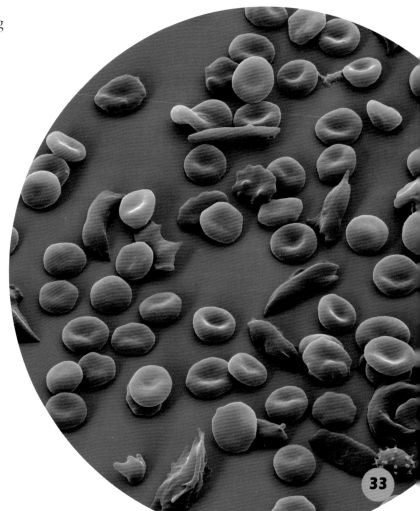

FUTURE PROOF

EGGS, SPERM and even embryos can be saved by freezing them to be used in later rounds of IVF treatment.

▲ Diane Blood eventually won permission from the European Court to use her dead husband's frozen sperm to conceive two children.

WHY DO IT?

Some medical treatments, for example, for cancer, can make people infertile. So couples may have eggs, sperm or embryos frozen to use when the treatment is finished. Tissues from the ovaries of girls as young as five can be stored for possible future use. Sometimes, a girl is born unable to produce her own eggs. As an adult, she may want children, and need donated eggs – which can be hard to get. In 2007, a Canadian, Melanie Boivin, became the first woman to donate eggs to be frozen and kept for her own daughter's use. Since then, several mothers have done this when illness strikes their daughters. Eventually the daughters may give birth to their own half-sisters.

ASKING PERMISSION

One big problem with these technologies is being sure that everyone involved agrees to it. A big news story in 1998 came when a woman named Diane Blood wanted to use frozen sperm taken from her husband before he died. She had to convince a court he had wanted this. She now has two sons, both born years after their father died.

But not all eggs, sperm and embryos can be used. In 2007, a woman named Natallie Evans lost her case in the European Court to use frozen embryos created with her ex-partner. She had had her ovaries removed as part of treatment for cancer but, before the operation, embryos had been created, using her eggs and her partner's sperm. After Natallie and her partner split up, her partner said he wanted the embryos to be destroyed. After a long legal battle, the court agreed he had the right to demand this – even though it meant Natallie could now never give birth to children.

▼ Natallie Evans was refused permission to use frozen embryos created by her and her ex-partner's sperm.

WHAT DO YOU THINK?

It is possible, in theory, for a woman to freeze eggs to use when she is older, so she can get on with her career. But IVF technology as we have it now is expensive and, as we saw on page 19, fails far more often than it succeeds. There is also the problem that an older mother is more likely to die before her child is grown up. Would it make more sense for employers to organise workplaces to make it easier for younger women to start families? What do you think?

WHAT IS A CLONE?

INSIDE the cells that make up all living things are "genes". These are strings of a chemical called DNA. This carries a code that tells the living thing how to grow and develop. When two living things have identical, or near-identical genes, we say they are "clones".

▲ This kitten, CopyCat, was the first pet to be cloned in 2002. Although she is a genetic copy of another cat, she is a different individual.

MAKING CLONES

Clones can happen naturally. As an animal embryo forms, it may split and develop into two nearly identical embryos. In humans, we say these are identical twins. Scientists have learned to make clones by splitting embryos, and implanting both pieces into mother animals, to develop into identical twins. Another way of cloning involves taking an egg from an animal and removing the nucleus, where the DNA is found. DNA from another adult animal of the same type can be inserted into the egg. The embryo from this develops into the clone of the animal whose DNA was used. This was how Dolly, a sheep and the first mammal to be cloned from an adult cell, was created in 1996.

WHY CLONE?

Cloning is useful in scientific and medical research. Scientists in Korea have created cloned Labrador puppies from a Canadian dog that was an especially good sniffer-dog. Less than a third of naturally born sniffer-dogs are as skilled as they need to be – but cloning could mean they will nearly all be. For dog-breeders, cloning prize specimens could be a way to make money, while some people want to clone pets who have died.

In 2004, a woman from Texas paid $50,000 for a clone of her pet cat Nicky, and in 2008 a South Korean company took a $150,000 order for a cloned pet dog. However, cloning is not a way to re-create a lost pet. The clone is just a different animal – as identical twins are two different people.

Cloning mammals is also a very complex and hit-and-miss process. Dolly was the first successful attempt to clone a sheep after hundreds of attempts. Many cloned mammals die before birth or are born with severe abnormalities. Even Dolly, who seemed to be a normal healthy sheep, had problems. She suffered from arthritis and died young from lung disease, although this may have been due to her unnatural lifestyle of living in a confined space. These factors have made scientists very wary of experimenting with human cloning.

▲ This diagram shows how animal cloning works in theory. Here, 15 embryos, each containing DNA from the same adult (01) are placed inside surrogate mothers, to create 15 identical animals.

▼ The last woolly mammoth died out around 10,000 years ago but some Russian scientists hope to recreate them.

FACING THE ISSUES

It is just possible that cloning could be used to bring back extinct species. In 2003, Russian and Japanese scientists announced they were hoping to clone a mammoth, using 200,000-year-old frozen remains. However, most scientists think that the DNA will be too old to use. Cloning might be a way of creating extra copies of animals at risk of extinction – but it is no substitute for protecting wildlife and saving habitats.

HUMAN CLONES

CLONING HUMANS is illegal almost everywhere. This is partly because it is dangerous and does not work reliably. More importantly, as a society, most people believe it is wrong to control what another human being will be like.

MYTH OR REALITY?

In 2002, a religious cult in the USA announced it had cloned human babies, but it was never proven. Supporters of human cloning see it as a way of living for ever – through the clone. But this misunderstands cloning as the clone would grow up to be a different person, with a different life and life-changing experiences.

Cloning complete humans remains only a theory, but this hasn't stopped writers of science fiction writing about it – including the idea of bringing historical figures back to life.

▼ Although identical twins are almost "clones" of each other, they are two separate individual personalities.

REAL CLONES

One kind of cloning is legal in some countries. This is therapeutic cloning – cloning embryos for use in medicine. Scientists in Newcastle were the first in Britain to do this in 2005. The embryos could be a source of stem cells to help treat certain diseases (see pages 32-33). When the news from Newcastle broke, Josephine Quintavalle from the organisation CORE (Comment on Reproductive Ethics) said: "No matter how it is created, a human embryo's destiny should be to live, and not to be turned into human stem cells."

However, not all scientists agree that embryos like these count as real people, and therapeutic cloning is becoming more widely accepted. In 2008, US scientists announced they had made cloned embryos using DNA from two adult men. This could be a step towards making stem cells with DNA exactly like individual patients – which could be very useful indeed. In fact, the technique has already been used with some success on mice that had a problem with their immune system (the system the body uses to fight disease).

WHAT DO YOU THINK?

In 2008, the UK government proposed allowing scientists to create embryos for medical use from animal eggs with human DNA inserted into them. Some people felt this was like making half-human, half-animal monsters, and were horrified. Scientists said that the objectors did not understand the technique – and that the embryos would never be allowed to develop, anyway.

● Debate this issue – with one side taking the point of view of the objectors, and the other as someone who hopes the research can help sick people.

► The 1978 film *The Boys from Brazil* was based on a story by the American writer, Ira Levin. It tells the story of a mad scientist who creates clones of Adolf Hitler (see previous page).

THE FUTURE

LIKE ALL SCIENCE, the research into fertility is making breakthroughs all the time. Some are simple discoveries – like finding out how important the health of both parents is to producing healthy children, and even grandchildren. Others are more complicated.

▲ We now know that good health means better fertility. This includes not smoking and not drinking alcohol to excess.

IMPROVING FERTILITY

For a woman who has had trouble conceiving, many new possibilities are opening up. If her womb is unable to carry a child, she may one day be able to have a womb transplant – like having a kidney or heart transplant. It may be possible to make an artificial womb, in which a developing embryo can grow. If a man's sperm is too weak to get into an egg, scientists have already found ways of injecting sperm into the egg. It might be possible to make sperm and eggs from other body cells in the future – or to take one egg cell and add DNA from another egg, to help make it more fertile. When an egg like this meets a sperm, it could create an individual with three biological parents – an idea that worries many people.

HELPING PREGNANCY

Tests to monitor developing babies are also improving. It is already possible to select embryos that do not carry disorders that may stop them from developing properly. Scientists are now researching ways of treating developing embryos that have inherited disorders with genes (sections of DNA) that can help make the baby – when it is born – healthy. The worry here is that some people may want to change the developing embryo even when it is perfectly healthy – in order to try to make it the kind of person they want it to be. This is called "enhancement", and is much more controversial.

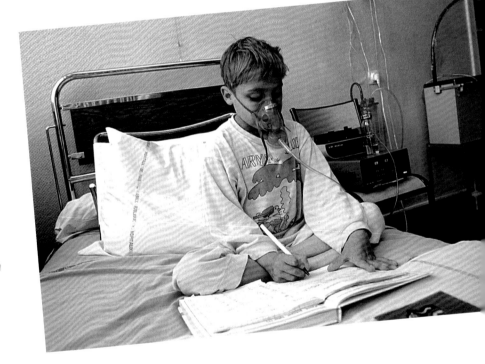

► A young patient with the inherited condition, cystic fibrosis. This makes breathing difficult and affects health in many other ways. Advances in science may be able to help these symptoms in the future.

WHAT DO YOU THINK?

There is the possibility of scientists actually creating the DNA for new forms of life. At the moment, the only DNA scientists have made is for single-celled bacteria – but one day they could make more complicated creatures. What problems do you think this could bring? Do you think this would be right – or dangerous, or wrong?

GLOSSARY

abortion Removing a growing foetus from a woman's body.

adopt To legally take responsibility for a child as if it were your own by birth.

ante-natal (before birth) Ante-natal tests can be carried out on a pregnant women to check on her health and that of her baby.

Artificial Insemination (AI) Artificially inserting sperm into a female.

Artificial Insemination by Donor (AID) When a woman has the sperm of a man who is not her partner put into her body using artificial insemination.

bone marrow The soft substance inside bones where blood cells are formed.

cell The extremely small basic unit that makes up every living thing.

cleft palate A malformation of the roof of the mouth which leaves a hole that needs to be surgically closed up in the baby.

clone A living thing that has almost exactly the same DNA as another.

conceive To become pregnant.

descendant We are descendants of our parents, grandparents, great-grandparents and earlier ancestors.

DNA Deoxyribonucleic acid, the substance of which our genes are made.

designer baby A baby born from an embryo selected for certain qualities.

egg-sharing Sharing eggs collected for IVF with another woman.

embryo An animal right at the beginning of its development.

fertility Ability to bear young.

foetus A young animal forming inside its mother or inside an egg.

gene A tiny part of a chromosome, made up of DNA, which influences what characteristics a living thing inherits from its parents.

immune system The system our body has for fighting disease.

In Vitro Fertilisation (IVF) Fertilising an egg with a sperm outside the womb.

ovary The part of a female animal where eggs (ova) are produced.

polygyny Having more than one wife.

saviour sibling A child born in order to help cure a sick older brother or sister.

sickle cell disease A disease where some red blood cells are the wrong shape.

sperm bank A place where donated sperm is stored for use in artificial insemination.

stem cell A kind of body cell that, unlike most body cells, can grow and develop into a range of different kinds of body cells.

surrogate mother A female who carries a baby for another woman.

thalassaemia A disease that affects the body's ability to create red blood cells.

therapeutic cloning Making cloned embryos of humans that will never be used to create a living person, but which can provide stem cells for use in medicine.

ultrasound Very high-frequency sound waves.

womb The part of a female mammal where young form and grow until they are ready to be born.

WEBSITES

BBC websites
http://news.bbc.co.uk/1/hi/sci/tech/859672.stm
This BBC website has questions and answers about therapeutic cloning.

http://news.bbc.co.uk/1/hi/sci/tech/2764069.stm
A BBC on-line news article about Dolly the Sheep.

The Science Museum
www.sciencemuseum.org.uk/exhibitions/genes/index.asp
The on-line exhibition about genes from London's Science Museum.

The University of Utah
http://learn.genetics.utah.edu/units/cloning/whatiscloning/
An informative site about cloning.

The Association for Science Education
http://resources.schoolscience.co.uk/abpi/new/resources/hormones/horm5.asp
A clear introduction for schoolchildren about pregnancy, hormones and IVF.

The UK Stem Cell Foundation
http://domain883347.sites.fasthosts.com/research/index.html
The UK Stem Cell Foundation's explanation of stem cells, and their potential for the future.

INDEX

Here are the lists of contents for each title in *Science in the News*: